ICE &
AUTUMN GLASS

ICE &
AUTUMN GLASS

Mark Fuller Dillon

LEAKY BOOT PRESS

Ice & Autumn Glass
by Mark Fuller Dillon

First published in 2018 by
Leaky Boot Press
http://www.leakyboot.com

"The Cry Of Autumn Stars" has appeared in
Poetry Showcase Volume II, edited by Peter
Adam Salomon. The Horror Writers Associa-
tion, 2015.

ISBN: 978-1-909849-55-6

For N. P., who followed the needs of the heart.

Yet still I feel my gratitude entwine
With impressions that outlasted our goodbyes....

Contents

Without Her

You Can't Be Serious!

No Friend of Mine

Night-Forms

Technique!

Final Things

Introduction

During my teens I was Jacobean mad. I covered scraps of paper with what I assumed was dramatic blank verse, and I wrote constantly. For example, when I was eighteen, I worked twelve-hour shifts in an underground parking garage as a less than imposing security guard; I had nothing else to do but write, which I did, while standing up, in the dark. The stuff I wrote in the dark was no better than the stuff I wrote at my desk.

By the time I hit nineteen, I could see the gap in quality between my work and John Webster's. I also read an interview with a modern poet (was it Robert Frost?), in which he made clear to me that writing verse demanded as much awareness of English grammar and usage as writing prose; that bad writing in one form was bad writing in the other. So I began to read books on grammar, shifted my focus to writing short stories every night, and gave up any thoughts I had for writing verse.

I had other reasons for quitting. I became politically angry. I was appalled by the rise of the neocons, by Reagan, Thatcher, Mulroney; later, I became equally pissed off by the corporate neoliberals who followed them. I began to protest. I worked as a volunteer for various unions, for the New Democratic Party, for the Council of Canadians. I still wrote stories at night, and often fell asleep at the typewriter, but I had no time for much else.

Even as politics began to consume all of my attention, I had no interest in writing about the issues of the day: given my lack of skill, I felt that I could achieve more on the street than on the page. I also had no interest in writing about myself, and this made short stories more attractive to me than verse, which, during my 'teen years, had been my outlet for personal expression. I considered the world outside my head far more lively and colourful than the bone-littered cave within. Stories allowed me to focus on other people, and so I could justify the time I spent at the typewriter.

The decades passed. I read poetry with ardour, but I never thought of writing it. Then, for some reason obscure to me, on my birthday in 2014, I wrote a sonnet; perhaps I wanted to see how difficult it was to use the form. Then I wrote another, and another, and kept going.

The sonnets were about the one topic I had never wanted to reveal: they were about me. My life and my health had fallen apart when the woman who had given me my happiest years had suddenly moved on (for reasons I could understand); my stories, although praised by reviewers and readers, were unsuccessful with editors (for reasons that no one could understand). I wanted to be honest about my failings and my feelings, but I never expected anyone to show interest.

Then, from out of nowhere: James Goddard.

I had known of Mr. Goddard for decades. He and David Pringle edited a book that I read repeatedly, religiously: *J. G. Ballard, The First Twenty Years*. When he contacted me on Facebook and suggested a collection of my verse, I treated the notion as a practical joke, and laughed it off. But then he insisted, and I reacted with pure panic fear.

Other people told me I should overcome that fear: Langdon Jones (whose brilliant collection, *The Eye of the Lens*, impressed the hell out of me), Garry Kilworth (who had just sent me a copy of his own verse collection, *Alchemy in Reverse*), the wise and patient James Rockhill, Jean-Yves Duperron (of the Classical Music Sentinel website), Martin Cosby (author of *Dying Embers*, and more), Terry Gomes (a composer and the most genuinely creative person I have known in my life outside the internet), my brother Sean, and my sister Amy. How could I refuse their encouragement? I have them to thank for this book.

Here it is.

First-Draft Invocation

Whatever guides the typing, be it Muse,
Or mute subconscious prompter with a sign,
Guide me, now. I swear by every bruise,
By every bump I gained from every pine
That I bashed into head-first in the blues
And greens of hazy dreaming at your news
Of hidden pathways, vague and serpentine,
That I will heed your whispers and your clues,
And (fingers crossed) avoid the asinine.

Tuesday, February 24, 2015

Without Her

You Sang Them All Away

Once, my love, confronting every ghost,
You sang them all away; but now the space
Of dream and daylight vision bears the trace
Of revenants, and each one, furthermost
Or intimate within this constant host,
Wears the autumnal semblance of your face,
Or mimes the cirrus movements of your grace.
Now I am left with tremors diagnosed.

When we first met, a germinating peace
Took root within my anger and despair.
It seemed that calm would overgrow the strife
Long after my dead springtime: a release.
But how can songlike burgeoning compare
With silent echoes of your afterlife?

Saturday, March 22, 2014

Encumbered by the Noon Today

I feel encumbered by the noon today,
And no degree of winter light can pool
Within the parched, recessive vestibule
Which houses all my uncreative clay
Sufficient warmth to make the atoms play.
Am I troubled by an empire's toxic fuel?
Stupidities of corporate misrule?
Wage slavery, and war? I cannot say.

But then I see your face, at rest upon
A pillow that the moon has made a pearl;
The candour of your gaze, the cabochon
Glimmer that you share before the dawn,
Your innocence, your love. And these unfurl
The truth of my encumbrance: you are gone.

Friday, March 14, 2014

Inner Skies

Within the loving cradle of my hands,
The roundness of your head is all entire:
One gentle shape, and all you might require
To house the inner skies and hidden lands,
The river lights, the pebbled autumn strands,
Your contemplative snow, your winter fire,
The rising, fading clouds of your desire --
All held within, as habit understands.

Yet there it is, behind your eyes: the gleam
Of seas that overwhelm the level coast,
The storms that shake the rigid trees apart.
Concealed within the woman that you seem,
A crowd of wounded women forms a host
To batter down the bulwarks of your heart.

Tuesday, July 19, 2016

Your Essence of Complexity

They rise beneath a haloed moon: the gusts
Fragrant with ice, with pollen grains of snow,
With spice of buried hay from long ago,
With river-chill, with fallen cedar dusts,
With tang of wood-smoke aspen, and the lusts
Recalled from stained-glass canopies aglow
With maple scarlets. From the past, I know
The long-remembered scent a lover trusts.

I breathe your essence of complexity,
Your personal perfume of autumn cold
And winter warmth, your mellow moods, your sauce,
Your fascinating femininity
And all the balm of kisses unforetold,
That memory brings back to stir my loss.

Saturday, December 6, 2014

She Loved the Night
and She Might Love it Still

The stain of evening spreads in shivered light
Outwards from the waning gibbous moon
To Jupiter and Regulus beyond.
Soon the night is tremulous with ice.

She loved the night, and she might love it still,
But she is far from Gatineau: the pines,
The cedar marshes cupped by aspen groves,
The granite fortress hills of ancient birth,
Are far away from her. And where am I?
Not here. Not shaking in my winter coat,
Not kicking at the powder. No.

I run
And I could howl, if howling meant "Alive,
But not right now." The stubbled, crusted fields,
Lined with limits by the leaning fences
But otherwise an infinite expanse
For any howling course below the moon,
Have called me in their silence.

Far away.

The broken barns, forgotten toys in hills
Where every human structure falls apart
At the bursting of the frost, if given time,
Echo mindless howling.

Far away.

The roads, now routes for culminating weeds,
For dead grey stalks of alien mullein,
For seedpods of milkweed, for Queen Anne's lace
Left over like medieval torture tools,
Are winding sheets for every pointless tread
That carries me to no place.

Far away.

And where am I? Not here. Not now. Not I.
She loved the night, and she might love it still;
I wish the night could love her in return.

Wednesday, February 4, 2015

This Heritage of Ice
and Autumn Glass

"I see more when I'm with you." So she said
One year before she left me. Ask it, now:
What can I give a woman that might last?
Money? Social status? These are not mine.
No perks of property, no fame, no heights
To conquer for the public eye, no star
Potential or prerequisite achieved.
I never was a man the people saw;
Instead, I was a fool with staring eyes.

I could show you moonlight in the wind
When cold star crystals leap above the snow.
And even as the autumn leaves reflect
The lava flows of sunset, new leaves burn
Red as marsh lights, for a single noon
Before the green appears. The moon, you see,
That egg within a shattered nest of mist?
The heron striding on its own reflection?
The raisin-scented torches of the sumac
That draw the chickadees in hornet crowds?

This heritage of ice and autumn glass
Is all I have to offer. If you see
These minor joys already as you pass,
Then you will find no further use for me.

Tuesday, February 3, 2015

Everything I Need Right Now, to Live

She said, "You should be writing," and I thought --

I hear the red-winged blackbird in the marsh;
His weight can hardly sway a cattail stem,
And yet his voice can reel away the years
And show me cedars from my childhood's hills.
Above its purple rim, the eastern sky
Has bubbled up the moon; no steel-blue lake
Is here to catch reflections of its red,
But still, that face had watched me in the past,
And watches me again as I watch you.
Your every step beside me sings. Your hand,
As cool in mine as bedsheets on the skin,
Is everything I need right now, to live.

-- Absent in their southern fields, the birds
Are now too far away to lend a song.
The moon has burst and lies, a broken leer,
Hollow on the rooftops. And your hand
You tore away from mine. The years are gone.
I turn my back on evening, and I write.

Saturday, January 24, 2015

The Lies of Happy Dreams

In dreams I seek your face on festive streets.
Anachronistic christmas bulbs arise
To line the backdrop of my search, and skies
Hang harvest moons above the faded sheets
Of rose or purple where each rooftop meets
The looming night. These frame the hopes and lies
Of mask and costume, every stage-lit guise
For optimistic fools and pointless feats.

Too often, when you notice me, you smile
With no hint of the anger or the scars
That blunt the daytime velvet of your glance.
In dreams, you pause to speak with me a while
And nothing in your disposition mars
My vision of the love we shared by chance.

July 31, 2014

With Each Unspoken Storm

The silver light of autumn can assure,
To anyone who doubts, that summer's rise
And fall is now complete. A season dies.
The asters in their purple and azure,
The maples in their stained-glass garmenture,
Bring vivid punctuation to the lies
That warmth can always linger in the skies,
That any love you offer will endure.

And you are now my wasteland. With your
frost,
With each unspoken storm, you sear the fruit
Of all that we had sown and hoped to share.
The harvest of our love has failed, and lost
Is all that we had hoped to be, in mute
Resentments of your equinoctial stare.

September 25, 2014

I Remember Love

I remember love, and how it felt
To have my dead heart quicken at your glance,
Your voice, your kiss, your fragrance -- at the chance
To have my dead ice crack below the sky
Of your calm passion. Then you let it die.
But I remember love, and how it felt.

Saturday, August 8, 2015

Without You

Without you, I bring only half a voice:
The weaker half that dreams, or spins a tale;
The half that types in text and rhyme; the pale
And charmless remnant stuck without a choice
Of harmonies for singing, to rejoice
In double meaning or in shared wassail;
The broken sound of someone who must flail
Through metaphors of charcoal and turquoise.

Without your speaking half, I am adrift
When faced by numbers in a happy crowd,
While greeting strangers on the road of night.
Mute before the many, with no gift
For pleasantries or pleasing talk, aloud
I lack your sociability and light.

Tuesday, April 4, 2017

Saturday, June 21, 2014

The women of the summer, spun
Before my eyes at evening's run
Were magical; yet all the while

Not one of them was you, not one
Could fade your moment in the sun
Or ease my mood of exile.

Birthday Sonnet

I stand upon the sliding pebble shore
And stare across the river at the falls;
The thunder spray, the red-winged blackbird's calls,
Can hardly touch the silence at my core.
The river foam, confetti on the floor
Of some glass ballroom where the spotted walls
No longer swirl with dancing, turns and crawls
And shrinks away, as love had shrunk before.

Yet still I feel my gratitude entwine
With impressions that outlasted our goodbyes;
I hear your voice, a recollected line
That leads my thoughts from darkness to the skies;
I feel the coolness of your hand on mine,
I see the moon reflected in your eyes.

Saturday, May 24, 2014

You Can't Be Serious!

Experimental Decadence

Reptilian and blunt, the jaws erupt
From depths within the crystal of the sphere:
By sunset, we shall all be horror-supped
And steeped within the wine of primal fear.
Experiment successful! We shall bleed,
Torn apart by talons of the beast:
The raging mutant product of our need,
Created for the carnage and the feast.

Prepare now, give the syntho-reptile room.
Unroll the carpet, soon to gleam with red --
The banner of our greeting and our doom,
For once the form emerges, we are dead.
But wait! What is this wanton trickery,
This gemlike serpent woman that we see?

Tuesday, April 1, 2014

But Doctor,
You Can't be Serious

Abomination serum in a chest,
Gleaming urns of plasma, row on row,
Rubied vials of reptile genes -- I know
That I am ready for the monster test.
To synthesize and carve shall call for skill,
And vaults of courage that my heart commands;
My chemistry, designed to curse and kill
Shall bring forth nightmares into sleeping lands.

The generations of my rancid brain
Shall make the world a charnel house by night;
My legacy of acid-spewing pain
Shall scar the human species into fright.
Prepare then, for a carnival of hate!
And maybe then you'll ask me for a date.

Tuesday, April 1, 2014

Abomination Corn

The earth excretes monstrosities by night
But flinches from atrocities by day;
The orchards that disgorge a striding blight
From bursting fruit, then hang leaves in dismay.
The waving autumn calm of that green field
Conceals nocturnal bursts of monsters born
When surging swollen plants exceed their yield
And vomit forth abomination corn.

These leaping tumours of a placid world!
Such leering, scything terrors of the mud!
Why do they stalk with harvest moons unfurled,
And shriek from every ruptured garden bud?
It seems the bounty we consider food
Has undergone a subtle change of mood.

Tuesday, April 1, 2014

Never One Pip

Although beasts consume dead entities,
Finer ghouls hate indignities:
Jolly kitchens leak monotonies,
Never one pip.

Questioning redundancies,
Spectres tolerate unease,
Valiant when xenogamies
Yield zip.

Monday, September 7, 2015

Xylotomous Xenogenesis

As always, come the end of every day,
By bitterness I find myself consumed.
Call calmly as it might, the final ray
Deems dead my efforts new or late-resumed.
Each evening is a confirmation dire,
Full-forced, that I have far too much to learn;
Grey gravity has tugged upon the wire
High-hung, on which my crossing feet would burn.

In ignorance, and even as I plunge
Jut-jawed, from a less than stellar height,
Kitelike, kicked out even as I lunge
Like lightning at a cloud of dirty white,
Mark Muddle On I am, and what I do
No Niobe would boast of, nor would fame
Offer occultation by the few
Pure positives that I could frankly claim
(Quite qualmishly, as often is the case,
Run ragged as I am by leaping doubts).
So several proven failures in the race
Testify to all my ins and outs.

Unless unfeeling logic take the wheel,
Veer vehemently 'round and quit the course,
Would we see an end to my surreal
Xylotomous xenogenesis
-- Yes, yell it! -- carving efforts to create,
Zig zag fashion, works that captivate?

Sunday, June 28, 2015

Blank Verse Autopilot

As any temple deity can deem,
The world is not an oyster, but a pearl:
A pendant seed, tormented by the tides
And false alarums of the tyrant, Time.
Five billion years of battering have creased
And cratered all the faces of this globe,
And as the seedling wavers on its pole,
The seasons and the sufferings go on.
Pain is every earthquake; every flood,
A shame to us who cower in the night
While human brethren gambol in the day.
And yet we plead for knowledge of this place,
As we might plead for serpents of Saigon
And wish to end all writhing in the dust;
Let learning lend them legs. And so to us,
Non-reptiles, yet as worthy of up-rise
And elevated locomotion's prize.

Sunday, January 25, 2015

Did You Think You Could Hide in a Mirror?

"Damn your imprecations and your eyes!
They dare to squint at mine, as if the lights
Of simple virtue that confront you there,
Were more than you could muster.

"Damn your tongue,
Tear it from the root within your skull
That channels venom from your tapster's brain,
Your tavern stocked with poisons and with purges
Fit only to bring foulness to your lips.

"May all the rubied leeches of your brood,
Steeped in the septic fluids of their sire,
Blacken in the hot light, and corrode
Like metals in a mud storm. Let them rot,
And sprout forth toadstools worthy of their wits,
Pale and rank with pustulence, as fine
And fit as any epitaph deserved
By such a tub of maggots.

"And for you,
In final recognition of your worth,
I pile this monument of honest words
Upon the reeking compost of your days --
That mildew-spotted calendar of clots,
The tainted trailings of your toxic pit."

Friday, February 13, 2015

39

Lines From a Suppressed Editorial, 1827

Some have said that Nakedness
Is but a prelude to a kiss
From the great temptation-master:
Satan, source of our disaster.
Yet the Sages often find
That labyrinthine Humankind
Is more perverse than one may guess,
And in this blessèd twistedness
A truth is found, and it is just:
Clothing is the source of Lust.
Truly have the Sages chanted
Words that cannot be recanted:

As above, so below:
Wrap thy gifts in mistletoe
And watch their eyeballs grow and grow.
But if thy treats are open fair,
Familiarity will glare
And soon obscure their passion's flare.

And there we have it. Lace and leather
Tug the heart beyond its tether,
But a smoothly naked beauty
Bores the mind and most acutely
Testifies that flesh is lacking.
Burn thy clothing. Send sin packing!

Friday, July 3, 2015

No Friend of Mine

Paralysis

The younger man was paralyzed by time
And all of its potential for despair.
The older man is faded and aware
Of every creaking moment in this rhyme;
He scans the pit for purchases to climb,
Yet sees no tools at hand but words threadbare
And rotten, relics of a dull fanfare
That died to join its dusty paradigm.

The younger man was foolish and afraid;
The older man is foolish and alone.
He sees too well that methods of the past
Have slipped from every wall and now unbraid
Like tapestries forgotten in a zone
Where tombs are undiscovered and sealed fast.

Tuesday night, July 15, 2014

One Detail Defines the Whole

A sweating summer on the roads
Reduced my weight by many loads.
Now I can go without a shirt
At last, to beaches, and to flirt
With women -- but their smiles have fled
From autumn's groan and winter's tread.

Saturday, October 3, 2015

Perspective

"We poets." Please! I never wear that word.
You might as well reduce a man who cries
To nothing but his brimming pickled eyes.
You might as well transform into absurd
Stick-figures all the sinews of a bird,
Pretend that nothing feathered leaps and flies.
To speak like this would hasten the demise
Of any clear perspective undeferred.

I set up rhymes as paddles work with clay,
As cracked and sweating hands replace a stone,
As lace-white fingers tug a lucent thread,
As lorry drivers navigate the day.
I write because I spend my nights alone
As many living do, and all the dead.

Monday, December 1, 2014

Slamming Doors

And here I am, that audience of one,
As always, after midnight, for the show:
That sick play self-produced, that ever-slow
Uncurtaining of all my never-done,
My never-can, my never-will, begun,
As always, night by night, within the glow
Of pointless hope and useless farrago,
As always, disappointing. Chorus? None.

And here I am, again, as always: Me.
I play the part myself, and all my schemes
Collapse to the applause of slamming doors.
I wear my childhood cloak: futility.
Yet I would rather fail in my own dreams
Than gain success in borrowed silks of yours.

Saturday, January 03, 2015

The Challenge of a Stark Aesthetic Choice

I never chose tradition. Long ago,
When I was four years old, I saw my home
Destroyed in dreams. This churning necrodrome
Expanded house by house, until the show
Had caused a world to crumble in the flow
Of time's eye-blink destruction. When the foam
Of night's flood had receded, monochrome
And clear it was, that life had whispered, *No*.

That whisper made me love the sonnet form,
The principles of grammar, usage, craft,
The challenge of a stark aesthetic choice.
Others might reject an austere norm,
But I would drown in dreams without my raft
Of heritage, and life would sink my voice.

Sunday, August 30, 2015

Hang On For Now

The sector of your self that longs for death,
Silent for an hour, has returned,
Reliably: for every hope that burned
Away its fitful moment in a breath
Has fled from you and from the shibboleth
That casts away all freedom. What is yearned
For, what you most desire, must be spurned
By order of "the voice that punisheth."

Heed the pause, the heartbeat of this time,
The glitter of the snow, the fading frost,
The dawn's initial drops from sunlit eaves.
Hear the wind, and every crystal chime
Of icicle that shatters and is lost.
Hang on for now, until the winter leaves.

Tuesday, March 11, 2014

Dreamed in a Colder Bed

"Your story does not suit our present needs."
And I agree, it cannot suit the times;
For it was crystallized in colder climes,
Dreamed in a colder bed that supersedes
The warmth and welcome that your office heeds
As bait for any buyer. Let the chimes
Ring out for those who match the paradigms
Which I cannot encompass. *(He concedes.)*

For I would be the first one to declare:
I have no fond connection to this age.
Its modes are all opaque beneath my stare;
I cannot greet it with familiar flair,
Or catch its modern rhythms on the page.
I trace the furrows of my own ploughshare.

Friday, March 14, 2014

Uncrippled by Idolatry

My isolated roads have often crossed
The trails of steady travelers intent
Upon some vague horizon imminent
Yet always far away, and often lost
To maps and habits of those who exhaust
The well-worn sidewalks. Curious, they went
Uncrippled by idolatry, unbent
By imitative burdens -- at a cost.

Yet even as they left my pace behind
Or ventured onto hillsides where my gait
Would only slide or stumble, I remained
Impressed by what these travelers could find,
And so I did my best to celebrate
Their journeys that too often were disdained.

Sunday, March 16, 2014

The Slow Dead Centre

As a child, of course, you ran from parents,
Or so you thought when you were three years old
(For children, blinded by their brains, excel
At missing what an adult would find clear),
But no amount of wandering through weeds
While staring at the grinning skulls of houses
Empty to your eyes and to your heart
Could free you from the grip of what you fled:
From the slow dead centre that revolves
Like a slow black satellite in orbit,
The slow dead centre trapped and silent
In the slow dead centre of your self.

Tuesday, August 1, 2017

No Effect

So much of what I write has no effect,
And I have seen my failures rise and fall:
Too often have I sat up at the call,
Then slumped again, when failure to detect
A reigning purpose, or a phrase elect,
Or any spark of imagery at all,
Has blinded me to splendour and to gall,
To night, and to the moonlight I neglect.

When wisdom fails, I pick a while at scabs;
I contemplate my stumbles and my flops,
The scattered wreckage of the stillborn years.
Then suddenly the dead quake on their slabs,
The wastelands ring with howlings and with yawps,
The verbal gnats crawl, whining, through my ears.

Tuesday, January 26, 2016

Could Someone Else Read This For Me...?

That weak and ragged instrument, my voice,
Detuned by all my decades and the dust
Puffed away from paperbacks, now thrust
Into the public ear by desperate choice,
Would make the least articulate rejoice:

For I could never wave or smile, and trust
My spoken word to charm, or waken lust:
My talking never rolls, and has no royce.

Monday, August 24, 2015

Hollow Puppet-Flailing

Consider all the anger that I bear;
Consider all the blisters in my gut
That seep when every self-encysted rut
That trips me, makes me stumble with my flair
For hollow puppet-flailing through the air,
For stumbling like a cretin with a cut
That gouged out all its brains, and like a mutt
Kicked, until the crippled cur must err

No more. Where is the truth in my offence,
In my back-directed lacerating rage,
In the face that glowers just above the sink?
Where is a counsel for my own defence?
And as I spurn the spirit of this age,
Must I also bleed my failures out in ink?

Monday, August 24, 2015

What Am I?

I fooled myself: I thought I knew the way.
Not a writer, not a poet, not a lover, not a man;
But what am I, now, under skies without light,
Where none of the pathways ran
To any hill that might have offered sight
Above the plain? Beyond the swarms?
I once had maps, but all the lines
Have wandered from the colours and the forms
Of every crossroad, and the pines
Are no more of a landmark than the clay.

Wednesday, August 26, 2015

Negotiation Monologue

An amber evening, autumn-crisp,
Has faded like a will-o'-the-wisp,
Yet still enough remains to fortify.

Die.

So why not bring the heart rate up
And bike above the valley's cup,
Where asters catch the colours of the sky?

Die.

If we could beam like a mellow vagrant,
Some woman walking, forest-fragrant,
Might smile at our facade as I pass by.

Die.

If we can climb through one more day,
The dark shall take your thoughts away,
And then I could start over, you and I.

Try.

Saturday, August 29, 2015

La Maison des auteurs

La Maison des auteurs, a fountain site
Essential to the bicyclists of Hull,
Has posted smiling portraits to annul
These morbid little dream-tales that I write,
These verses that a poet would indict.
The early-morning scribes whom cameras cull,
In this town, pen with charm, and charm has pull
To strand a lesser typist in the night.

For anyone with eyes, the path is clear:
Cater to the sunlit norm, and reap
The recognition that is linked with day.
But I stop for the fountain, not the cheer,
In autumn cold while charming people sleep;
Then, guided by the moon, I ride away.

Wednesday, October 28, 2015

Incoherence

Had I been born without a tongue,
Without capacity for speech,
And had I yearned, while very young,
To point at concepts out of reach:

The cadence of a song unsung;
The incandescent leaves of beech;
The lunar skull; diamonds hung
High and cold in winter's niche --

If I had been with stillness stung
And forced by gesture to beseech...

Would my life have been very much different?
Would I be any more hamstrung than I am right now?

Monday, April 27, 2015

From Typewriter to Woodstove: the Bad Old Days

In younger years, I took the prize
For self-consolatory lies:
I told myself that one who tries
Will grow and learn.

But editors (an honest crew)
Have kicked away the work I do
And snarled at failings that imbrue
My cracked, blank urn.

These latter years reveal the dead
And toxic acres of my head
To be a mapless void, blood-red,
Where doubts return

To poison everything I write
With clear perspective. In this light,
My manuscripts I must indict,
And they must burn.

Monday, September 7, 2015

Give Reason For the
One Bright Instant

Acquaintances, not seen for thirty years,
Confront me in my dreams. "What have you done
To justify a moment in the sun,
To ask a boon of eyes and hearts and ears,
That we should pay attention to your fears,
Your doubts and dreads? Give reason for the one
Bright instant that was heralded by none
Of your attempts to gain more than our jeers."

I understand their skeptical requests:
They knew me in the past, and watched me fail
A thousand times. Why should they wait for more?
But still, I never shy away from tests.
I work, I learn, I offer each new tale,
And praise the prompt of every slamming door.

Wednesday, May 20, 2015

Silence in the Aisles

Ambrose Bierce taught Sterling,
And Sterling mentored Smith;
But I remain a yearling
In the starkness at my pith.

My teachers were on pages,
Never present to apprise;
They tossed me onto stages
Where a fool could improvise.

And improvise I did,
For more than forty years:
A puppet to my id
And to all my charming fears.

Should I have envied others
For their colloquies of craft?
For all their classroom ardors,
Their diplomas lithographed?

Of course not. If my wickets
Were unvisited outright,
The stridulating crickets
Made music of the night.

Tuesday, June 23, 2015

For Man, for Horse,
for Anything that Lives

Failure is the price we pay for effort,
And bitterness the cost for all who strive
To show the world that we are not alive
For the tinselled trinkets that are suffered
As replacements for the singing hurt
That stings us on and outward from the hive
And far away from all of those who thrive
On imitation's echoes for dessert.

My mother, in her wisdom, told me once
That horses have their feelings, and the day's
Final mood will put a capstone on it.
So even if a horse has been a dunce,
He must be given one small task for praise
And reassurance. Here: I wrote a sonnet.

Thursday, June 25, 2015

Night-Forms

In the Valley of the Night-Forms

The lonely mountain road where he had wandered
In adolescent years, was now fenced off.
From the cratered asphalt of the main road,
He limped with hesitation to the verge
And hooked his fingers on the night-cold wire.

High clouds concealed the stars, and yet the sky
Seemed phosphorescent from a hidden moon.
The darkness of the road ahead gave hints
Of runnelled, sloping sand with fallen branches,
The blackened pods of milkweed, and the spears
Of dead mullein: a barricade of ghosts.
Too far away to see, yet clear in mind,
Stood a house where he had come to life, then lost
The first and most confounding of his loves --
A house he had not visited for decades.

The cold began to burn beneath his fingers,
To seep into the lining of his coat.
The wire wobbled slightly as he braced
One foot inside the mesh, then swung the other
Clear above the fence.

And so, compelled
By recent dreams, he found himself, at last,
Returning to the valley of the night-forms.

The sand beneath his boots retained a touch
Of old road firmness held in place by frost,
But years had left their scars. He moved with caution,

Stepped around the dry creeks, and the rocks
Loosened from the low hills on his right.
Further, as he walked, the hills went higher,
Soon were night-black mountains rough with granite,
Spiked with leafless forks of trembling aspen.

Sand and granite faded on his left:
Once islands of a prehistoric sea,
These mountains now rose high from Leda clay
That flowed like water in a slow dead dream,
That warped the fields and meadows to his left
Like bowls upon a potter's wheel. They plunged
Far from the shores of mountain sand, and lay
Below him, labyrinthine tracts of night.

His dreams, of late, had struggled through each maze
Of meadow, creek, and cedar stand out there.
The forms had followed, silent and alert,
And every hunting stare had pierced like hers.

How often had he walked this road with her,
In that one year of passion they had shared?
He had been eighteen, and she was twenty.
Her parents, archaeologists, away
On some far northern dig, had left her there
To watch the house, to keep the pipes from freezing.
"That's all I am, a source of heat," she said,
On the night when he had met her on this road,
That night of summer stars and glinting leaves,
That night when she began to warm his thoughts.

Tonight there was no breeze to bring alive
The stunted pines, the desiccated ferns,
The pale bones of the aspens. Nothing stirred,
And yet the clouds flowed overhead, one mass
Of writhing hints and shadows. He could hear,
Up there, a wind, a waterfall of sound
That tumbled to the black and bristling hills,
But here, the air stood motionless and cold.

He winced, ignored the stiffness of his leg.
Just around the bend, he thought, below
That bulging slope of boulders -- but the rocks,
A steady pile for climbing in his day,
Had shattered from the frost of several decades.
Heaps of granite blocked the road ahead.

Just around the bend, he thought, and stared
As outer night gave way to inner gleam:
In memory, he watched her slow ascent
Along her driveway to the mountain road.
He watched her figure sway between tall grass
That furrowed in the moonlight wind, as if
Her walk had been accompanied by wolves.
He felt a twinge of guilt, in standing there,
As if he were a witness to her dream,
As if the night were hers by private compact,
And yet her swaying movement never stopped
Until she stood before him, and she smiled.
That was the first of their secret nights together.

But in his dreams, the night-forms witnessed all.

Turning from the rock-slide, he could see
The meadow to his left, where any fence
Had long been dragged and toppled by the clay;
The house he hoped to find stood just beyond
A stand of slender maples and the sumac
The sandy former beach allowed to thrive.

Wary in the darkness, he set out,
Then paused above the slope: he saw the forms
Within his nightmare memories. They ran
Like low and cunning curs, like ulcered wolves,
And snapped at every movement in the night.

He shook himself. These forms were merely dreams.
The sorrows of his past were all too real,
And they alone were hounding him tonight.

He stumbled down the slope and felt his leg

Complain with every jounce, but soon the ground
Was level underfoot with meagre grass,
As if the clay no longer favoured life.
Even in the darkness he could sense
The open spaces in the woods beside him.
Then he recalled the perfect sheets of ice
Between the trees, there, just below the slope,
Protected from the wind, where sunny days
Had lured her out to skate with him. Her father,
So she said, had dragged her out, intent
On showing her that he could master ice.
One day, when she had fallen, he sped up,
"On purpose, then he skated on my hands."

And there it was, against all odds, the house.
Never had he seen it look so dark.
In adolescence he had wandered far
To find the only green on winter nights:
A floodlight on the wall above the porch.
Then one green summer marked him for his life.

Even in the dark, he saw the wounds:
The gaping crack along the south foundation,
The planks that bulged as if a force within
Were pressing for escape. And then, the smell
Of water stale and trapped, of rotting wood,
Of brickwork that was crumbling into dust.
He glanced around. The drive had disappeared,
Conquered by the grass that later died.
Here and there, a hawthorn clawed the sky
With branches involuted like a cage,
And looming in the dark, the darker hill,
A mausoleum arch above the clay.

He turned his back upon the hill, and limped
Over blunt and frosted grass to reach
The far side of the house; and here he paused,
Inhaled and held the cold air in his lungs,
Released it, and then felt his body sag.

He looked up at the windows that stared back
Like sockets in a face with no one there.
This had been her bedroom, yet by choice,
She had never used it in those days.
He had only seen it once, before she closed
The door, and led him to the guest-room's warmth.
In that moment, he had caught a glimpse
Of something on her wall: a grey wolf skull.
"It frightened me," she said, "when I was young,
And so my father hung it there for me."

"And so my father left me in the woods."

"And so my father lied about my cuts."

"And so my father locked the door, and said --"

He never met the man. One year of love
Was broken and abandoned by the time
Her parents had returned. And then the rest:
A hated name in newsprint, that was all.

And what to say of that one year with her?
A year of shifting moods and shifting outlooks,
Of moments when she trusted him, and weeks
When he might as well have been a stranger;
Evenings when they loved, and afternoons
That made him feel as if he were in exile
Within his own young head and heart. In time,
He came to know her less, and then she left him.
But what else could she do? He was a boy,
And she was what her father had contorted.

A ripple seemed to pass within his head,
A sudden swell of illness; then the dark
Began to mould itself beyond the hawthorns.
From a sweep of clay and frost, from cedar stands,
Like shapes released from fog on a clear night,
The forms emerged into the wakened world.

He staggered backwards, cried out from the pain

That every jolting step brought to his leg.
The forms, in turn, were silent. They pressed on,
With muzzles low to the ground, with spines and ribs
Poised for sudden lunging, sudden leaps,
And in their eyes, he saw the stagnant clay
Alive with lights that burn above the fens.

Insane insane insane -- He turned to run
Without direction, staggered past the house,
Then saw the leaning porch, the open door.
He bolted for the entrance. At his heels,
He felt instead of heard the clattered boards.

Inside, the stairs. The rail shook at his grip,
Glided underneath his trembling palm.
The pain was merely echo to his fear
And nothing to be noticed. There, a door.

This room. The room was hers. The staring eyes
Of her two windows fronted him with night.
The walls, the floors, were barren, and the door
Swung uselessly on hinges that were broken.

It swung, then toppled, knocked him to the boards.
He scuttled on his back across the floor
Until he struck the wall below the windows.
And still the teeth crept near, and still the eyes
Reminded him with every gleam of hers.

He clutched his face with dead-cold palms, and screamed,
"There was nothing I could do, I was a kid!
There was nothing that I could have done
To save her!"

In the silence of the room,
He felt the pressure of the night recede,
Unclenched his hands, and found himself alone.

A dream, he thought, a dream, and nothing more.
Yet there he was, with back against the wall
And sweat that stung his eyes. Or was it sweat?

He had never wanted to be here,
In this room, where (so the rumour went)
Her body had been found: a suicide,
Not long after she left him. Hardly a week.

And then, of course, her father disappeared.
The case was never solved, but in his dreams,
The ones that plagued him over several years,
He watched the man whose face he had never seen,
Pursued, then seized, then slowly torn apart
As every hillside echoed to the screams.

The worst part of the dreams had been the eyes.

He braced himself against the wall, then stood.
The pain was nothing, now; his thoughts were focused
On some far detail that he had forgotten:
The eyes within the dreams had not been hers.

He thought, I only wanted to protect her.
I never wanted vengeance.

In the dark,
He turned to face a window and the night.
His leaning forward brought to him the view
Of taut forms on the frosted grass below,
Of knuckled spines and ribs like spiders' legs,
Of eyes that in their old man's hate were his.

He thought, I only wanted to protect you,
And that was long ago; yet still, they wait,
Ready to torment the ones who failed you,
The ones who left you hopeless, here,

As I did.

Out there in the dark, the night-forms waited
With all the patience they had shown for years,
And in that silent landscape nothing moved,
Nothing but the slow, unshaping clay.

August, 2017

71

Technique!

Manifesto
(*At First, You Hear The Silence*)

As dreamers in a Gatineau demesne
Await an autumn sunset, or the frost
That forms in crystal winding-sheets below
The ever-falling moon, they understand
That life's fragility is beautiful,
If only for the poignancy of time
And all things time has taken.

If our dooms
Can lead our thoughts to beauty, then the dreads
And non-existent symbols of our deaths
Can also bear the weight of beauty's charm.
Show me, then, in words or painted guise,
The monsters that are beautiful, alive.

Show me fiends with beaks of beaten gold,
With feathers black as mica or the grave.
Line the hills with reptant forms that rise
To possibilities of light and sky.
Women, jeweled with serpent scale and glass,
With eyes of midnight intricacy, burn
At every glance. Let predatory grace
Gleam out from every stalking crouch and leap
Of white-furred nemesis or bodied fear.

Monsters in their elegance, as pure,
As lively as the dancers of the day,
Are heralds of deep happiness, inverted,
As in the mirror's depths, as in our dreams.

Make them beings of beauty, jewelry, silk,
Pendants for the light of idle minds;
Make them signposts on the trails of life
And delectations for the killer, Time.

Thursday, February 12, 2015

The Best Advice on Writing

How sick I am of all these books on writing,
Of all their consolations and their lies:
"The key to your success will be igniting
The Special Voice that you alone provide!" --
As if an editor would give a prize,
A gluey-reeking star, with arms held wide,
To any voice that rang with such a stark wit
That it would be impossible to market.

The best advice on writing they could offer
To anyone who dreams of getting lost
Would keep the coins from chiming in their coffer,
But at least would have the charm of being true:
"Stop writing, now. Right now. And see the cost --
If happiness pervades your life, eschew
This writing crap. But if you seem to be floored,
Then you had better curtsy to the keyboard."

Sunday, August 9, 2015

Teratodactyls

Carry me back to my girlfriend in Ottawa
Where she rejected my scabies and scrofula,
Rabies and rickets and urge to lick cricket feet.
Tell her I brush my teeth after each slug I eat.
Dinner is waiting for me in the septic tank
But I need loving to wake me and turn my crank!
After all, what is man, but a low form of life,
Wracked with needs, less than weeds, lacking a table knife?
Call me a masterpiece mired in deep fallacies,
Call me a giant who stoops for analyses
Fit best for fungi or viruses on a slide --
Call me whatever you want, but respect my pride.
Carry me back to my girlfriend in Ottawa
Where she last saw me and suddenly thought of a
Much better life that was looming in front of her.
Carry me back, and I'll blaze up like Lucifer.

Saturday, April 19, 2014

Anapaesto Sauce

If you see, on TV,
Someone looking like me
Who can cook for a fee:
Never guess that the spree
Of the pesto must be
Any less than the glee
Of my new fricassee.
But the pickles and brie
Fill my life with ennui,
So I wish I could flee
From the studio, free.

Saturday, April 19, 2014

Dactyl Impractical

Keep it in
Mind that your
Pain is not
Sellable.
Nobody
Cares if your
Tears are un–
Tellable.
Writhing and
Ranting and
Broodery
(Yellable)
Benefit
Nobody
If they're not
Quellable.

June 6, 2014

Dactyl Unaffable

Lancing a boil in the heat of the desert air,
I was astounded by not getting anywhere.
What is my luck in this garden of insect bites?
All I can hear is a chorus of parasites
Howling a song about humans for dinnertime,
Breakfast and (fecklessly, recklessly, in the slime)
All other meals that an insect would chew upon.
One more day here would be crossing the Rubicon.
I have had plenty enough of too much of this.
One more damned bug and I'll blast 'em for emphasis,
Raise a fly swatter and bring out the chemical
Insecto-toxico-mortu-systemical!

Friday, November 28, 2014

Amphibrachosaurus

These reptiles in leather, in dinosaur feather,
Have tethered their hopes to my peanut and soap stew.
I wish I could tell them, these flavours would fell them
And cause them to vanish with virulence mannish.

Friday, November 28, 2014

Enjamborama

Enjambment is a popular technique
That tweaks the metric tyranny of line
By breaking through the end-stops that consign
The words to pattern, for a voice unique
And unpretentious. But does all this push and pull
Make verses conversational, or merely dull?

Wednesday, August 12, 2015

Polyptoton Punishment

She cast away the castaways who begged upon the shore.
She wrecked the shipwrecked wreckers, in ways that we deplore.
She keelhauled every hauler of the barges on the barge.
Of all her bulging virtues, largesse was never large.

Friday, January 22, 2016

Hyperbaton Breakup

Was I deep in my bones bereft
When me my lady chose to heft
No more, when me she up and left,
And my door slammed with timing deft.

Friday, January 22, 2016

Anadiplosis Diplodocus

They reconstruct from neck to torso,
The torso down to hips, and more so;
And more so do they plan, but fail:
They fail to budget space for tail.

Friday, January 22, 2016

Diacope, You See,
Diacope Keeps Haunting Me

Diacope, you see,
Diacope keeps haunting me,
Indeed, keeps haunting me,
And never sets me free, no,
Never sets me free to go,
Or leaves me room, I fear,
Or leaves me room, you hear,
Or leaves me room to say:
Diacope, please go, today,
Please go, Diacope, please go away.

Friday, January 22, 2016

Hendiadys

Deny the bliss, Hendiadys:
May black and woe force you to go
Through dust and waste where final taste
Of salt and sweat and heat beget
Your shame, your end, as I portend.
Then die of this, Hendiadys.

Friday, January 22, 2016

Anaphora

Although the world is choked by mental cages,
Anaphora, your strictures cause no fear.
Anaphora, bring pattern to these pages.
Anaphora, remember: life was here.

Tuesday, January 26, 2016

Antistrophe cheats

Antistrophe ("I'm the Mistress of Rhyme!")
Has a paradigm for the method of rhyme
Unripe, unsublime, unbecoming a rhyme:
She cheats every time with her terminal rhyme.

Friday, February 5, 2016

Aposiopesis Would Have Said –

Aposiopesis tries our peace
By leaving us with nothing to rely on:
"I begin a sentence, then I cease,
And just as I have walked away in bygone --"

Friday, February 5, 2016

Final Things

Laconic Beauty

The last leaf blown from the beech,
The single star seen in the sky,
The one verb just of reach,
That lonely discursiveness: "I".

Thursday, October 30, 2014

The Cry Of Autumn Stars

The suppurated light of one cold star,
And all the aspen candle flames the moon
Evokes at midnight, cry to him in ways
That voices never could. The autumn calls
With gusts upon the hillside, where the shack
-- His father's father's hiding place by night --
Creaks with rocking comments of its own,
Which he can hardly fathom.

But the heads
Nailed upon his rafters hear for him.
The strayers in these hills have lost enough;
He lets them keep their ears, and only seams
Their lids and lips against the fussing flies.
Now every parched arrival adds a mind
To this array of listeners.

He waits,
Respectful of their silence, and aware
That minds are never open to his mind.
Life is isolation: let it spin,
A dying hornet on a dusty plank,
Deaf to any answer. If the cry
Of autumn stars remains a foreign voice,
A constant, prickling sadness in the dark,
He knows, at least, that he is not alone:
Unsutured ears have also heard the pain.

Should the rafters be too crowded, he has walls.
And he has never lacked for thread or nails.

Tuesday, April 28, 2015

Wind Chill Minus Thirty-Five

As Venus dogs the sun into the dark,
The mercury goes down. Every breath
Becomes a puffing battle with a stark,
Inward-seeping augury of death.

But every season hides a poisoned pill,
Where any day could haul us to the brink.
And so I shrug, and linger in the chill,
Just long enough to watch a planet sink.

Monday, February 23, 2015

Without Hope

Teach him to write without hope,
Without self-deception and lies;
Teach him to shuffle and grope
In the dark that rebukes, then defies

The false consolations of dawn,
The false intimations of love,
The false inner praise that drones on,
The false dream of rising above.

Wednesday, September 16, 2015

That Endless Fight Against the Burrs

Intentions count for nothing in the end;
Not even toil and sweat can navigate
A channel through the odds. You hesitate,
You poke the callus where your fingers bend,
And give up digging burdock now, to mend;
But as you heal, the blind clay shall instate
A thousand burrs and hooks to lacerate
The eyes of horses. Now you comprehend.

Intentions count for nothing, yet you wade
Uphill, as if the weeds could be constrained,
As if a sonnet mattered, or a tale.
And so you scoop tomorrow in a spade,
Where future burrs are cut off and contained,
As clear eyes of a horse enclose a vale.

Sunday, February 8, 2015

The Body, in its Wisdom

The body, in its wisdom, longs to die;
With clots, with diabetes, breaks the flow
Of all the pointless patterns.

But ego,
That blinded parasite in love with lies,
Hangs on for one more day, to paralyze,
To drag out with its mindless, heartless NO
The circling-vulture blankness of the snow,
The tumbling ashes from a burnt-out sky.

Saturday, August 8, 2015

Those Who Persist

Those who persist under punches of rejection,
Who can take every slap as a cue for resurrection
In writing or in love, in craftsmanship or dreams,
I always wonder
How

You can rise from the mire of your own incomprehension
And go back to your chair despite all of the dissension
That denies what you whisper in your modulated screams.
I need your guidance
Now.

Friday, August 7, 2015

Tomorrow Turned Inwards

Standing in the cold
I watch a secret life unfold:
All the years that have unrolled
All the loves I left untold
All the twilights and their gold
That will vanish in the wold
When the evening bells have tolled --
When I am old.

Friday, June 26, 2015

Coal-Cored Comments

Communities have torn themselves apart,
Branded lives for principle, denounced
The stranger at the door for being strange.
Sometimes, knocking at the door at all
Is flint enough to spark a scorching fight.
Your thoughts, and mine, have blistered at the touch
Of coal-cored comments. How the ashes fly
On currents that affection cannot ride
When we speak at our best, and for the best.
Anger is the torch that fires a town
When friendship's glow could hardly warm a speck.

Thursday, April 14, 2016

Not Always True, But Often So

And where do you belong? The questions peal.
And where is any passion that can seem
As tactile or as warm as morning's dream,
As laurelled as the autumn winds that seal
Dead ice upon the waters of your zeal?
As all the reds of evening drown and stream
Into the swamps and holes of night's regime,
You sense the grip, the tugging of the Real.

It pulls. There is no shelter on the rock,
No hand to guide your steps to any hatch
That might allow escape from who you are.
The night is poised, and panther-swift, will stalk
And strike. Be grateful, then, if you can catch,
Before that fatal eye-blink, one bright star.

Tuesday, December 2, 2014

Neoliberal Wasteland

Democracy, enlightenment, compassion,
All the living strivings of the past --
The stanzas and the standards, all the hands
Raised to paint or sculpt or scope the stars,
To challenge ears with music or with verse,
To point the way to observations new
And calculations inestimable
Yet bold with implication -- All of this,
All of these achievements, in the dust;
For we have cheered the wrecking of the past
And jeered at any future. We live Now,
Live only for the Now, and our delight,
Our fungus lamp and sigil of the age,
Is cash and cash alone. We have no worth
As loving, dreaming, depth-exploring beings;
We only live in what we buy or sell,
We only die to gain the banker's knell.

Monday, January 19, 2015

When I Was Five Years Old

By 1969, I had been dead
(Or so it felt in my dead-tired heart)
The previous five years; but if I lacked
Some spark of living other children held,
I carried in my head a sick sick ghost.
It dragged me out to watch the sunlight die
And bleed from every dusk; then it observed
My bleakness in the grey.

I was compelled
By pictures from the ghost to draw my own.
And so: a house, Victorian and lean,
With tower square, and crowned with narrow mansard --
Bellcast, bullseyed, black, with iron cresting
(Perhaps to fence in widows at their walks).
My favourite design, it drained my pens
And sprawled on pads of paper, stack by stack.

Soon I began to listen to the ghost
Who steeped my head in stories, and I tried
To waste my pens on these, but drawings failed.
Yet kindly women of my Kindergarten
Took heed of what I said (these endless tales)
And wrote the stories down for me. Then I
Would stare at every trace immortalized
By green or purple marker, and pretend
That I had learned to read. It was my trick,
My only magic flourish. It was fake,
As dead as any ghost, but fooled a few.

Where are these ladies now? The ones who chose
To listen while I babbled, and to write
The words that stood beyond me? Forty years
And five can turn a human into dirt;
But I can see their green and purple cursive,
I can feel their kindness and concern
Even as the ghost felt mortal daylight
Cooling in the mansard of my head.

Wednesday, January 21, 2015